XTREME SCREAMS

THE WORLD'S MEANEST
Monsters

A&D Xtreme
BOLD HI-LO NONFICTION

An imprint of Abdo Publishing
abdobooks.com

S.L. HAMILTON

TAKE IT TO
THE XTREME!

GET READY FOR AN XTREME ADVENTURE!
THE PAGES OF THIS BOOK WILL TAKE YOU INTO THE THRILLING
WORLD OF THE MEANEST MONSTERS ON EARTH.
WHEN YOU HAVE FINISHED READING THIS BOOK, TAKE THE
XTREME CHALLENGE ON PAGE 45 ABOUT WHAT YOU'VE LEARNED!

ABDOBOOKS.COM

Published by Abdo Publishing, a division of ABDO, PO Box 398166, Minneapolis, Minnesota 55439. Copyright © 2022 by Abdo Consulting Group, Inc. International copyrights reserved in all countries. No part of this book may be reproduced in any form without written permission from the publisher. A&D Xtreme™ is a trademark and logo of Abdo Publishing.

Printed in the United States of America, North Mankato, MN.

032021
092021

Editor: John Hamilton; Copy Editor: Bridget O'Brien

Graphic Design: Sue Hamilton

Cover Design: Laura Graphenteen

Cover Photo: iStock

Interior Photos & Illustrations: Alamy-pgs 34-35; AP-pgs 16 (inset) & 30-31; Cartoon Network-pg 41 (bottom); Dave Rubert-pg 44 (inset); DC Universe-pg 37 (bottom); Getty-pgs 9, 21 (inset) & 26-27; Gustave Doré-pg 36; Hanna-Barbera-pg 41 (top); iStock-pgs 1, 4-5, 8, 14-15, 18-19, 20-21, 22-23, 24-25, 37 (background) & 44; Legendary Pictures-pg 39 (inset); NASA-pg 1 (Moon); Radio Pictures-pg 38; Scholastic-pg 37 (middle); Science Source-pgs 16-17 & 25 (top); Sega-pgs 42-43; Shutterstock-pgs 6-7, 10-11, 12-13 & 28-29; The History Channel-pg 40; Toho Co.-pg 39; Warner Bros-pg 42 (inset); Wordsworth Editions-pg 37 (top).

LIBRARY OF CONGRESS CONTROL NUMBER: 2020948034

PUBLISHER'S CATALOGING-IN-PUBLICATION DATA

Names: Hamilton, S.L., author.

Title: The world's meanest monsters / by S.L. Hamilton

Description: Minneapolis, Minnesota : Abdo Publishing, 2022 | Series: Xtreme screams | Includes online resources and index.

Identifiers: ISBN 9781532194856 (lib. bdg.) | ISBN 9781644946237 (pbk.) | ISBN 9781098215163 (ebook)

Subjects: LCSH: Monsters--Juvenile literature. | Monsters in mass media--Juvenile literature. | Monsters in popular culture--Juvenile literature. | Monster films--Juvenile literature.

Classification: DDC 398.2454--dc23

TABLE OF
Contents

CHAPTER 1
THE WORLD'S MEANEST
Monsters

Monsters are described as big, frightening creatures that attack humans. Most are created in legends and stories. But some are thought to live in the wild. People wonder if they are real or **imaginary**.

XTREME FACT

Cryptozoologists are people who search for creatures that have not been proven to be real.

CHAPTER 2

History

When people began exploring the world, they encountered creatures they had never seen before. Some maps warned: "Here be dragons."

PACIFIC

ATLA

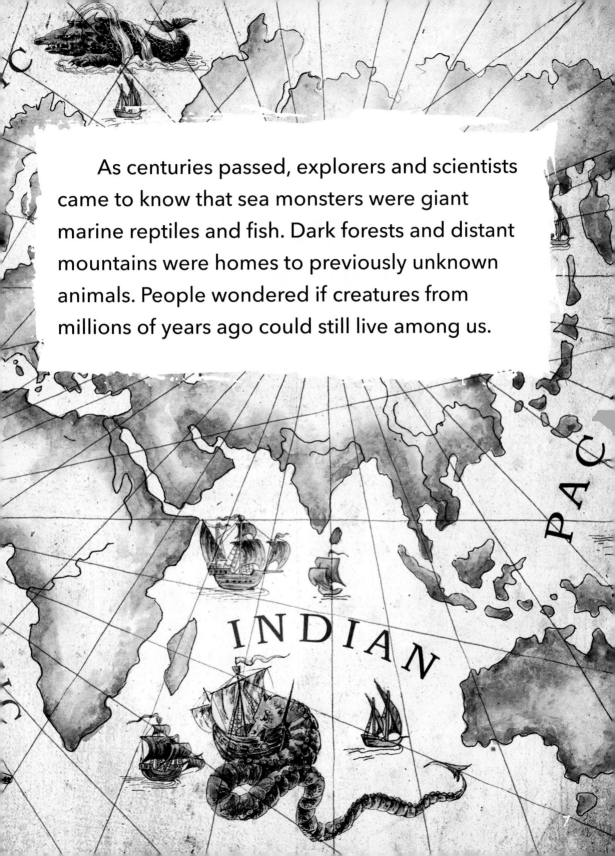

As centuries passed, explorers and scientists came to know that sea monsters were giant marine reptiles and fish. Dark forests and distant mountains were homes to previously unknown animals. People wondered if creatures from millions of years ago could still live among us.

CHAPTER 3

Monster Sightings

Caution
Sasquatch
Sightings

Protect Your Park
No Tree-Cutting
Or
Trail-Building

Hundreds of people claim to have seen a furry, apelike creature. Known as Bigfoot, or Sasquatch, it is said to hide in forests and swamps of the United States and Canada. None have been brought back, dead or alive. Other than blurry photos, there is no proof this monster lives.

XTREME FACT

Bigfoot is described as 7-10 feet (2-3 m) tall and weighing up to 500 pounds (227 kg). People also say that they hear a grunting or screeching sound and smell a horrible odor.

A still frame from a 1967 film shot by Bigfoot-seekers Roger Patterson and Bob Gimlin. People thought it was real until Bob Heironimus came forward 35 years later. He was hired by the two men to wear the Bigfoot suit. The footage was fake.

From the Himalaya Mountains come tales of a humanlike monster known as the yeti, or Abominable Snowman. Many explorers have searched for the **elusive** creature.

Giant footprints have been discovered in the snow. Some thought they were made by a yeti. Scientists believe the tracks were just distorted animal prints that enlarged by melting and refreezing.

A 1951 photo of a giant footprint, taken by explorers in the Himalayas.

For centuries **mariners** told tales of a giant sea creature called Leviathan. It made the sea boil. Steam hissed from its nostrils and clouds of smoke rose from its mouth. Some thought it was a monster. Others believe it may have been a blue whale. Adults weigh 150 tons (136 metric tons) and spout water 40-50 feet (12-15 m) in the air.

Blue whales are the largest animals on Earth.

Norse myths tell of the kraken. The huge creature could **engulf** and sink an entire ship. Sailors feared a kraken's attack. Some thought it was a sea monster, while others believed it was a giant octopus or squid.

In April 1934, a doctor took a photo of what appeared to be a sea creature swimming in Scotland's Loch Ness. The deep lake would be a perfect hiding place for a long-necked marine reptile. Some thought it was an ancient **plesiosaur**.

The Surgeon's Photo, as it was called, seemed like proof that Nessie lived. However, at the time, many people thought the image was an otter or marine bird.

The search for "Nessie," the Loch Ness monster, went on for decades. Finally, in 1994, it was discovered that the photo was actually a toy submarine fitted with a clay sea monster head. Many people still wonder if some kind of sea creature is living in Loch Ness's dark waters.

Many cultures have tales of dragons. Mexico's Quetzalcoatl is a winged serpent-god. Europe's legends tell of Saint George killing a dragon that demanded **human sacrifices**. Asian dragons bring good luck and are thought to be kind and wise. The stories may have arisen from fierce, real reptiles.

Quetzalcoatl

Dragons have many different looks. Some have two legs and some four. Some fly with magic and others with wings. Some breathe fire or poisonous gas. Some are good and others are evil.

Saint George kills an evil dragon.

19

Africa has stories of a monster with a long neck, an alligator-like tail, and the body the size of an elephant. It is called Mokele-mbembe. Its name means "one who stops the rivers." Some believe it to be a **sauropod** dinosaur. Others say it's an elephant swimming with only its trunk and the top of its head showing.

A swimming elephant may look like Mokele-mbembe.

XTREME FACT

In 1992, a Japanese film crew flying over Lake Tele, Congo, captured 15 seconds of what they thought might be Mokele-mbembe. The blurry film shows something leaving a large V-shaped wake as it swam.

Kongamato is described by African natives of western Zambia as a beaked, flying reptile. Some believe it to be a pterosaur, a creature that died out 65 million years ago. Reports of a flying demon with a wingspan of 4-7 feet (1-2 m) and a mouthful of teeth continue to make people wonder if the monster really survived the ages.

Pterosaurs had arms and bodies covered in stretched skin. Some think the flying reptile might have survived to modern times.

Chupacabra is a mysterious monster seen in Puerto Rico, Mexico, Nicaragua, Chile, and the southern United States. Some say it has sharp teeth, red eyes, and pointed quills running down its back. Others believe the monster may have been a stray dog, an aye-aye, or humans playing **grisly** tricks. Still, some claim chupacabra is real.

Chupacabra means "goat sucker." It was named when an unknown creature drained the blood from several dead goats.

The rare aye-aye is native to Madagascar.

CHAPTER 4

Real Monsters

Some "monsters" are really just monster-sized animals. Many snakes grow to amazing sizes. One record-breaking python measured 49 feet (15 m). That's longer than a city bus! Pythons have even been known to consume children and small adults.

Reticulated Python

A Komodo dragon hunts for prey using its forked tongue to pick up chemical molecules in the air and on the ground.

Indonesia's Komodo dragons are the largest living lizards in the world. They can grow as big as 10 feet (3 m) in length. They eat all types of meat, from eggs to water buffalo.

These real-life dragons are deadly. A bite from a
Komodo dragon sends huge amounts of **bacteria** into
its prey's bloodstream. This causes death within a week.

Giant squid live deep in the ocean, but sometimes come to the surface to hunt food. These huge creatures can grow up to 50 feet (15 m) in length. They have been known to attack small ships.

A real giant squid hangs in Paris's French National Museum of Natural History. It is preserved with a special resin.

XTREME FACT

Giant squid are so big they have been mistaken for floating islands.

The giant Pacific octopus is the largest species of octopus in the world.

The largest recorded giant Pacific octopus weighed 600 pounds (272 kg) and had an arm span of 30 feet (9 m) across. With 2,000 powerful **suckers** and a biting, parrotlike beak, it is easy to see how **mariners** might think of them as sea monsters.

CHAPTER 5
MONSTER HUNTING
Equipment

A thermal image of someone in a Bigfoot costume shows how a heat-detecting device can help locate a monster.

People look for **elusive** monsters all around the world. Some search in remote areas and many use heat-detecting devices. The most important equipment is a video or still camera to clearly document the creature.

CHAPTER 6

MONSTERS
In the Media

Monster stories have been told for centuries. Whether from authors' **imaginations** or real-life creatures, books are filled with tales of wild beasts.

One of the earliest books, *The Bible*, tells of God destroying a Leviathan.

In 1869, science fiction author Jules Verne wrote *Twenty Thousand Leagues Under the Sea*. His tale of adventures and sea monsters is still read today. It has been made into comic books, movies, and games.

R.L. Stine's Goosebumps HorrorLand series has several monster stories, including *Creep from the Deep*.

The DC Comics series *Gotham City Monsters* features hero characters from Monstertown, including Frankenstein, Killer Croc, and Orca.

Monster movies bring adventure and scares to viewers. RKO Radio Pictures' 1933 *King Kong* was one of the first major monster films. The 25-foot (8-m) -tall gorilla was called the "Eighth Wonder of the World." The famous monster continues to star in movies, books, and games.

XTREME FACT

In the 2017 film *Kong: Skull Island*, King Kong was 100 feet (30 m) tall. That's taller than the tallest dinosaur that ever lived.

Godzilla was created for a 1954 movie. Awakened by atomic testing, the giant, lizard-like monster attacks a city in Japan. Godzilla has been in so many movies, it was once the longest-running **film franchise**. *Godzilla: King of the Monsters* came out in 2019, and more movies are planned.

The original Godzilla's special effects are called "suitmation." Godzilla was a man in a reptile suit destroying a miniature city.

Monsters are seen in many TV shows. The History Channel's *MonsterQuest* searched for a variety of creatures. Cartoon monsters are sometimes fierce and sometimes friendly.

MonsterQuest searched for information on monsters, such as Mothman.

Jonny Quest took on a yeti and other monsters in the 1964-1965 series.

In *Monster Beach*, a brother and sister go to an island occupied by quirky, surf-loving monsters and an evil witch doctor with tiki minions.

Video games often feature fearsome monsters. In some, players fight the evil creatures and in others, they are the monsters. The skills and challenges are fun and exciting!

Rampage first came out in 1986. Players control one of three monsters: a werewolf, a lizard, or a giant gorilla.

Players of *Jurassic Park: The Lost World* video game fight their way through
many monster dinosaurs that inhabit the isle.

CHAPTER 9

Are Monsters Real?

Many people claim to have seen monsters. But most have turned out to be fake. Without bodies, bones, **scat**, or tissue samples, it's impossible to prove. Clear photos or video footage helps. What is seen in the dark, or in rain or fog, can trick a person. Most monsters are fictional stories.

Stompers used to create Bigfoot tracks.

XTREME
Challenge

1) What phrase was printed on early maps to warn sailors of areas where sea monsters might be found?

2) What are two names for a furry, apelike creature that is said to live in North America's swamps and forests?

3) A Leviathan is a sea monster that sailors feared. What do scientists think it really was?

4) What kind of monster is a kraken?

5) Scotland's "Nessie" was photographed in 1934. But what was really in the doctor's Loch Ness photo?

6) Name two dinosaur-age monsters that people think might still be alive in areas of Africa.

7) What fictional monster was called the "Eighth Wonder of the World"?

8) What would be proof that a monster is real?

Glossary

bacteria – Single-celled organisms that multiply rapidly and break down living tissue. Bacteria often cause sickness, and sometimes death, in animals and humans.

elusive – Someone or something that is hard to find or catch.

engulf – Wrap around or surround something completely.

film franchise – A series of related films all produced around a central character or characters.

grisly – Something awful that causes horror or disgust.

human sacrifice – The killing of a person or persons as an offering to a god, spirit, ruler, or supernatural power, in order to protect the rest of the people or tribe.

imaginary – Not real. Pretend.

mariner – A sailor.

plesiosaur – A long-necked, small-headed sea reptile that swam in Earth's oceans 200 million to 65 million years ago, during the Mesozoic era. The name plesiosaur means "near lizard." When first discovered, it was thought that the bones were from an ancient lizard.

sauropod – The largest of the plant-eating dinosaurs. They lived during the Mesozoic era, from about 245 million to 65 million years ago. As the biggest land animals to ever live, they weighed as much as 100 tons (91 metric tons) and stood more than 40 feet (12 m) tall.

scat – Animal droppings or poop.

suckers – Shallow, cup-shaped organs that hold fast to an object. An octopus's tentacles have rows of suckers that are used to hold and taste their prey.

Online Resources

Booklinks
NONFICTION NETWORK
FREE! ONLINE NONFICTION RESOURCES

To learn more about the world's meanest monsters, please visit **abdobooklinks.com** or scan this QR code. These links are routinely monitored and updated to provide the most current information available.

Index